Building Personal Wealth

A Personal Finance Guide for Small Business

Owners

Amarachi Stanley-Duru©2021

Dedication

To all Small Business Owners struggling to figure out how to build a business, even questioning why you started in the first place.

We're in this together!

Together we shall take territories and create generational wealth!

Free Ebooks

In order to say a 'Thank You' for purchasing *Moving From Idea to Profit*, I offer this book to you in appreciation. Unlock the secrets of personal wealth with this Business Planning Workbook.

Your journey to financial success begins now!

>Click here to download the eBooks NOW!!<

CONTENTS

Why do I talk Personal Finance?

Growing up in a city, arguably considered the commercial hub of the South East in Nigeria, I witnessed the rise of the most influential entrepreneurs of the 90s' in the Eastern part of the country. They were first-generation millionaires who had built their businesses ground up with grit and sweat. Some of them were the pioneers in the areas of businesses in which they were invested. Their businesses traversed various sectors of the economy, nationally and internationally recognized brands in transportation, logistics, manufacturing, import/export, production, education, agriculture, oil and gas etc.

These businessmen built great empires in business. Their personal lives demonstrated wealth and flamboyance. They were honored at every event that mattered. They excelled in philanthropy and their humanitarian activities earned them recognition and chieftaincy titles. They were celebrated as the people's heroes.

I wish I could continue my tale as a narrative on how these entrepreneurs enjoyed decades of prosperity, with details of how they built sustainable businesses and created trans-generational wealth. A good number of them succeeded yet a significant number didn't survive past the first decade.

Sadly, I observed as a number of these

seemingly thriving businesses went bankrupt over an average period of 10 years and the massive factories and warehouses turned into junk yards.

More disturbing for me was how "quickly" these great pioneers lost their personal wealth. It appeared their personal wealth was totally encapsulated in their business finance. Simply put, they did not have personal wealth, they literally lived off their businesses. Could this be the reason these empires failed? Let's leave that conversation for some other time.

The loss of financial stability after having experienced life as a multi-millionaire can be devastating. This was the experience of a personal friend and I imagine most entrepreneurs who've been down the same road probably have related experiences. Men who were known to be wealthy and powerful lost their status and influence as their financial power was gradually eroded as a result of a change in economic policy, poor business decisions, and in some cases change in consumer behavior and market trend, not forgetting governance issues.

But the real question here is, "Should a business owner lose his wealth just because his business experienced a downturn?

I witnessed this happen first-hand to a wealthy family member. An accomplished entrepreneur, he struggled to meet personal and family financial obligation owing to short-term challenges he faced in his business on account of changes in consumer behavior and market trends. This individual's experience in particular drove home for me the significance of Personal Finance Planning for Entrepreneurs.

Finance Planning for employees is relatively easy and straight forward. For most employees, they earn a fixed amount of income on a regular basis. They can most of the time conveniently make plans on their income because of the predictability and regularity of the inflow. On the other hand, for most entrepreneurs, there are significant fluctuations in their revenue which affects their net income. Mostly because they do not have a regular or fixed income, entrepreneurs find it a bit more challenging to plan their personal finances. This is especially so because when the business is just starting off most entrepreneurs suffer the fear of the risk of running down their businesses financially, and are therefore resistant to the idea of taking any form of financial compensation from their business.

Should a business owner pay himself?

I visited a dear friend in her business office and she during our conversation she blurts out, "Amy, you would have to help me figure out how to have my own money from this business". I honestly thought she was joking but it turned out she wasn't. She had been running an 8-figure business for over a decade, yet everything she had was the business and the business was her. She made personal expenses from the business. She didn't have personal funds. The business was the "general pot" from where everyone dipped their hands for food.

Unfortunately, not long after our conversation, the business fell on hard times and eventually failed. The result of this on the financial status of my friend was quite predictable considering the circumstances at that time. Within just a couple of months, things went downhill. Life became really tough. It became difficult to meet basic living expenses not even considering other obligations.

When businesspeople are starting out, there's usually the challenge of not taking a salary or any form of compensation from the business. This is mostly justified by obvious facts especially when the business is struggling to survive and like a demanding new born needs as much resources as can be pulled together. The risk with this approach of managing business finance is that it leaves the entrepreneur with an unconscious bias that the money in the business is belongs to him. But then the first rule of finance in business is

"Always separate your personal finance from business finance".

But the entrepreneur would ask, "I started this business with my money. My life savings, all I have is invested in this business. How dare you say that the business money isn't my money?

Valid question, indeed! This mindset begins to form the reason why entrepreneurs are strongly advised to take some form of compensation from the business, either as salary/wages or percentage profit sharing. Some of the reasons why an entrepreneur should pay himself are:

- There is a special feeling that comes with getting paid for work done especially when it is from your own venture. It acts a form of incentive and you feel motivated to do more. The reward may not equal the contribution made but every entrepreneur needs that motivation.

- It helps the entrepreneur make the distinction between himself and the business as an entity. Every business owner needs to register the fact that the business exists as a different entity even when that business is runs as a personal brand.

- It gives the business owner an idea as to how much money he has personal funds and if the entrepreneur chooses to reinvest the funds into the business or credit to himself as the owner of the business, he is certain of how much his income is.

- When you keep business savings aside from your personal savings you can tell what the liquidity state of your business is.

- Separating business and personal finance is one of the ways of revealing to the entrepreneur the true financial position of the business.

- A business owner has a better organized business when he is able to set up a proper payment and accountability process to maintain financial propriety in his business.

- Separate personal and business accounts are important for accounting and tax purposes.

- Investors and other regulatory bodies view the entrepreneur as committed to the business when his business and personal finance are separated.

How Should I Pay Myself?

Some schools of thought are of the opinion that the business owner should only pay himself out the business profit. Now, if the business is the only source of income for the owner, how then is he supposed to meet his personal needs if he only gets paid when the business makes a profit. What happens when the business does not make any profit? For some businesses it would take a while before the company can break even. Does this mean that through this period of 3 – 6 months or even years, the business owner would have to borrow to meet his needs?

On the other hand, one could ask, did the entrepreneur cover the other business costs – fixed costs and variables (utility bills, rent, power, fuel, maintenance, and staff). If he did even when the business didn't make any money, why would he fail to pay himself salary or take compensation from the business as this is also a part of the business cost?

I was privileged to pioneer the take-off of 2 business offices branches for different companies in the course of my career. The first business office was able to break-even in a little over 12months while the second recorded its first profit in a little less than a year. Interestingly, for the entire period while my team and I struggled to break-even, staff salaries were paid promptly, utility bills, vendors and suppliers were paid and every cost incurred in the day-to-day running of the business was settled to ensure the business progressed.

The true position of a business is only

discovered when you review the financial records and all business expenses should be captured in the financials including compensation for the owner of the business.

The point here is that as an entrepreneur you need to understand that salaries are a part of your business operating cost and must be included in order to determine the true position of the business. Therefore, if a business owner pays employees salaries, he should pay himself no matter how little. Where the entrepreneur fails to take a compensation, he creates a gap in the determination of the true position of the business financial situation.

How Much Should I Pay Myself?

Having established that the entrepreneur has to compensate himself in order to have his personal funds separate from the business, how does the business owner get to determine what his compensation in the business should be? In other words, how much do I pay myself?

In determining how much to pay yourself as a small business owner there are a few questions you should ask yourself.

- What is my business structure? Is this a sole proprietorship or are there other shareholders?

- What is the current financial position of the business?

- What does the business cash flow look like?

- How much will I take without putting the business under undue pressure?

- How much pay will take care of my basic living expenses? How much do I need to pay myself to get by?

- If I were working for another business how much would they pay me?

- How much pay will equate the duties I perform or the number of hours I put in?

After considering these, there are different options to choose from for entrepreneurs on how to get some form of compensation from their business. Two of the commonest options are:

1. **Pay yourself what you are worth in the business.** So this basically means paying yourself what you would have been paid if you were hired to work for some other company on the same role, in the same capacity in which you act in your business plus a little more. A little more because of the added responsibilities of entrepreneurship.

If you choose this option, you must understand that salaries are a significant part of your business operating cost therefore as a startup, consider the impact of this cost on your business financial position. Whatever the value of this cost, understand that as the business grows there is always room for making adjustments to your pay. The tricky part is that when you make upward adjustments to your pay, you also drive up the overhead cost of the business. A business owner once asked me during a business planning workshop if she could pay herself two salaries considering that she is doing the work of both Production Manager and CEO. I found that very interesting and my response was,

"Understand the financial situation of your business especially at the early stages. Consider that you may need to reinvest into the business for it to grow." Having the full picture of the implication of this decision will help you to either factor this cost in from the very beginning or note that this cost adjustment will be made in the future and make provision for it.

2. **There is also the option of taking a "lean pay".** This implies that you pay yourself a certain amount just enough

to take care of your basic living expenses. This is usually the first option for most entrepreneurs who are just starting out their businesses and have no other source of income besides the business to compensate themselves. This option requires that the entrepreneur be detailed and explicit in his estimation of what his living expenses are. How much exactly would you need to cover your basic living expenses? Expenses include rent, food, medical bills, utility bills, transportation, clothing, and other miscellaneous expenses. This exercise is more detailed that it appears and can be quite a daunting task but believe me if you would like to estimate a proper compensation for yourself and spare your business, you would have to do this exercise being sincere with the figures you assign each of your expenses. Now, that you have an estimate of your basic living expenses, you may go further to review the cost by examining your current living circumstances, what do you absolutely need to survive and provision can be made for unforeseen circumstances. When you work out these details you may now draw on this cost as compensation, your "lean pay" from the business.

It is important to mention that if your business is going through a crisis, you may need to reconsider the payment option you have chosen and ensure that you do not take too much money from the business. It would also be morally wrong if you pay yourself but do not pay your employees on the excuse of financial difficulties in the business.

Knowing exactly how much in figures it is you should pay yourself is dependent on what stage the business is at and the cashflow position of the company. There's no hard and fast rule as to how determine how much you should pay yourself. Different entrepreneurs handle this differently. Some decide on certain percentages from their profits and so their salaries fluctuate, other stick to a fixed amount no matter how well or poorly the business does per time. No matter what you decide, the financial situation of the business should not be compromised.

How do you pay yourself from the business?

There are 2 major ways in which a business owner can pay himself, one is a Monthly Salary while the other is through Drawings.

1. **Monthly salary:** Put yourself on payroll and get paid alongside your employees. We have already discussed how you can determine how much you should pay yourself. Putting yourself on the company's payroll helps to condition your mind to delaying gratification from your business to a particular date. It helps you schedule spending and manage financial obligations. It also

helps with tax management.

2. **Drawings:** This requires taking out a certain amount of bulk funds drawn from either the business profits or your equity contribution in the business (the money you invested to start the business) to finance your personal interests or obligations. Some entrepreneurs take their drawings quarterly, half-yearly or annually. The idea behind the interval is to ensure that the money is substantial and sufficient enough so the entrepreneur can invest it in a tangible personal project as a reward from their business investment. For some it is targeted at recouping their capital investment into the

business as it grows. Interestingly, there are some entrepreneurs who take both monthly salaries and annual drawings from their businesses.

Whatever option you choose, the goal is to ensure that as an entrepreneur you learn

- That your business is a different entity from yourself
- That your business money is different from your personal money
- How to make the distinction between the two
- Not to use your business money for personal expenses

The above outcomes have been the

cause of the failure and poor growth of several small business. They are not the only issues but when issues around business finance are corrected and we are able to ensure the business still has its "life blood" (cash flow), every other matter can be corrected in time.

Planning Your Personal Income

Now that you have money which can be considered as your personal income we can go ahead and set financial goals and plan your finances. It is important to do this so that you have a stable financial position away from your business so that in the event that the business fails or goes through a major setback, you, the entrepreneur is able to survive until you are able to bring around the business or pivot.

Steps in Planning Your Income

1. Determine Your Financial Position

If you seek to improve or manage your financial situation you must make an assessment of your finances the same way you take stock of inventory in business. A simple process involves confirming the following:

- What are your obligations?

- How many dependents do you have?

- How much you have as liquid asset (savings, fixed deposit, investments in financial instruments- mutual funds, stock, bonds)

- How much you have in real estate (residential, commercial, land)

- Other income generating income assets

- Calculate the size of your indebtedness

After you have determined these values, take away the value of your indebtedness from that of your assets. The result is known as your **Total Net worth** while the breakdown is the picture of your current financial position.

2. **What is Your Money Behavior:**

- What is your opinion of the value of money?

- Are you a giver, spender, saver or investor?

- What is the first thing that comes to your mind to do when you receive money?

- How do you behave when you have excess and when you have little money?

- Where or on what do you spend most of your money?

After you have successfully determined your financial position, you may want to look at your spending habits, if you could have been worth more and if you have managed your resources well. Do you believe money is meant to be spent, saved, shared or invested? Whichever, your opinion, it has a direct effect on how you handle money. Therefore, where is your money going versus what are your financial needs? This is a very critical exercise and you need to do this before your proceed to the next step in planning your finances.

3. Set a financial goal

Now that you know the state of your finances and probably what behaviors got you there, you may want to set financial goals in order to secure your future. Your goals could be short term (1 year and below), medium term (below 5 years) and long term (above 5 years)

It is however not enough to set goals, you must have SMART plans to achieve your goals. There are a few basic considerations when setting a financial plan.

- Service your debt portfolio by creating a repayment plan.

- Never spend all your income. Set a savings rule of 10% -20% depending on how much disposable income you have.

- Create and work with a budget. It doesn't make you frugal but helps you take charge and keep track of your finances.

- Set up an emergency fund. This a portfolio of funds that you support your basic living expenses for a minimum of 6 months should you run into sudden change in circumstances.

- Consider getting an Insurance Policy. This helps with covering costs which could arise as a result of medical expenses, losses due to theft and other unforeseen circumstances.

- Create an investment plan. There are so many option, local currency and foreign currency. You could talk to an investment advisor and get help with the option that suits your financial goals.

4. **Identify and evaluate alternatives**.

After you have set financial goals and possibly set up plans, it is important to make room for fluctuations and changes that could happen. There could be changes in the economic policies by the government which could affect the economy of the country. Your personal life circumstances could change from maybe singlehood to married life or you could have more children or dependents. Your earning power or source of income could change and this ofcourse could affect your financial goals and plans. Therefore, keep an open mind to create alternatives in the event of change in circumstances.

5. Implement financial plans.

Take prompt action in implementing your financial plans. Timing is of the essence when making financial decisions. Be sure to have an investment advisor or financial coach walking you through this process. Do not underestimate the value of an expert's advice.

6. Review process regularly.

Review your plans regularly. What worked 2 years ago in the market may not give the same results at this time. The world is moving at a fast pace and so are the changes in the global economy and the financial markets. Therefore, whatever plan you choose, savings or investments, do not ignore your portfolio. Although some investments are made for the long term yet you have to pay attention to the market so you know when to make changes to your portfolio.

Take an Assessment

Let's see how much you know about your financial status

* What is your level of education?

* Are you maximizing, effectively and efficiently deploying the value of your learning?

* How long have you been working or doing business?

* How much is your annual income (including allowances and bonuses for salary earners)?

* How much do you have in savings?

* How much do you have in liquid assets? And what kind of investments are they? (eg. shares, stocks, mutual funds, treasury bills, fixed deposits, bonds, pension)

* How much do you have in real estate (land, built up properties including commercial)

* How much is your residence worth? (Rented, Lease, Owned)

* How much do you earn as passive income?

* How much do you owe as debt?

* How many dependents do you have?

* What things constitutes your major expenses? You could make a list of your monthly, quarterly or annual expenses.

* What percentage of your income covers these expenses? What do you have left after these expenses?

* What is your financial goal for the next 12months?

* What is your financial goal for the next 5 years?

* What is your financial goal for the next 10 years?

* How do you hope to achieve your goals? Write down an elaborate plan on how to achieve this.

* What changes do you need to make in your behaviour with money to achieve your financial goals?

Personal Finance Planning for Small Business Owners

This resource is published by Amarachi Stanley-Duru

Business and Personal Finance Coach

You can visit my website

www.amarachistanley.org

for more resources.

Book a Free Consultation on Personal Finance Planning by clicking on

https://calendly.com/amarachistanley/personal-finance-planning

You may also reach out to me on +234-8039312042

Connect with me on social media

Facebook: @amarachistanley2

Instagram: @amarachistanley